AMBERLEY PUBLISHING

Having fun with Mokes: Holding on for dear life during a Moke run in the Lake District in 2011. (*Pat Douglass*)

First published 2013

Amberley Publishing
The Hill, Stroud
Gloucestershire, GL5 4EP

www.amberley-books.com

Copyright © John Christopher , 2013

The right of John Christopher
to be identified as the Author of this work
has been asserted in accordance with the
Copyrights, Designs and Patents Act 1988.

ISBN 978 1 4456 0919 5

British Library Cataloguing in Publication Data.
A catalogue record for this book is available from
the British Library.

Typeset in 9.5pt on 12pt Celeste.
Typesetting by Amberley Publishing.
Printed in the UK.

Small Car, Big Fun!

'Is it American?' This question from a member of the public was not unreasonable given that the focus of our attention was a vehicle which, in its coat of Spruce Green, bore more than a passing resemblance to a US Army Jeep. To be fair, the Mini Moke is a rare enough sight on British roads nowadays and unless you were once one of the pretty young things who pootled up and down London's Kings Road in the swinging sixties, or are a devotee of a certain cult television series from that era – no need to mention the name as you are reading this after all – then you will be forgiven for not recognising one. Moke owners have heard a lot worse during the car's almost half century of existence, usually along the lines of whether it is actually allowed on the roads or, more commonly, is it a kit car? The respective answers being 'yes of course' and 'most definitely not'. Finding the right words to sum up what the Moke is all about is both very difficult and very easy. Radio 2's Dermot O'Leary, for example, once described them as 'motorised roller skates'. He wasn't too far off the mark, and other suggestions have been, a) a flying bedstead, and b) a tent on wheels.

It would be fair to say that this confusion of identity arises partly because the Moke came into this world as one thing, a lightweight rag-top intended for the British army – a sort of mini Land Rover, if you will excuse the deliberate pun – but found a more enduring role as another. When the British Motor Corporation (BMC) launched it on the civilian market in 1964, they described it as a 'rugged run-about with a thousand uses', and indeed the impractical and uncomfortable little Moke did go on to serve in a bewildering array of roles ranging from golf caddy to police car, even as a pick-up truck for builders or farmers,

In this BMC press photograph of an Austin Mini-Moke the solitary windscreen wiper has been removed, presumably for a cleaner look. A few years of evolution later and we have the distinctly beefier-looking Australian-built Californian, shown *below* in this recent photograph of a hire car on Magnetic Island, just off the coast of Queensland. (*Rene Wachter*)

AUSTIN mini-MOKE

rugged run·about with a thousand uses

Original BMC brochure for the Austin Mini–Moke. Car buyers in the UK had the choice of either Austin or Morris models, depending on the dealership. The only difference was the badge and the colour of the brochure – *see page 18.*

but its core purpose remained constant: the pursuit of fun. And when talking Mokes, 'fun' is the one word that crops up time after time.

In 2011, when the *Wheeler Dealers* programme took on the Moke as a restoration project, presenter and former car dealer Mike Brewer started his assessment by saying that more creature comforts were to be found in a prison cell, but he was soon won round. 'Its middle name is "fun",' he managed to exclaim through teeth clamped tight against the biting cold. 'It is masses of fun to chuck about – and I want one.'

Top Gear's Jeremy Clarkson, the dark lord of automotive put-downs, also took a Moke for a spin through the streets of London. Inevitably, he began by reciting some of the car's quirkier qualities. 'Driving the Moke was, and is, noisy, uncomfortable, bouncy, draughty...' (All true of course.) But even he couldn't suppress a grin as he delivered his final verdict to the in-car camera. 'If you like driving Minis, and let's face it who doesn't, you're going to love this. It's alfresco fun in an anodyne world!'

THE MORRIS MINOR
TWO- AND FOUR-DOOR SALOONS

The Issigonis family tree: *Above*, a Morris Minor shown in a 1951 advert. *Right*, the Morris Mini-Minor, which was also sold as the Austin Seven before becoming universally known simply as the Mini. *Below*, a publicity photograph of Alec Issigonis beside one of the legendary Minis.

"QUALITY FIRST"
MORRIS *MINI-MINOR*

Who would have thought it possible... four adults travelling in comfort in a car just 10 feet long... with heaps of luggage... at up to 70 m.p.h. *and* 50 miles per gallon? But today Morris make it possible! With one stroke of genius they have turned the engine East-West *across* the car – and created the Mini-Minor, the roomiest high-performance small saloon in the whole history of motoring!

**IT'S WIZARDRY ON WHEELS AND
'QUALITY FIRST' ALL THROUGH**

Twelve Months' Warranty and backed by B.M.C. Service—the most comprehensive in Europe

MORRIS MOTORS LTD., COWLEY, OXFORD. LONDON DISTRIBUTORS: MORRIS HOUSE, BERKELEY SQUARE, W.1

Military Manoeuvres

Forever cast as the quintessential fun car of the swinging sixties, the Moke's intended purpose was in fact the exact opposite: it was militaristic. The Moke's inception dates back to the 1950s, when the British Motor Corporation's designer Alec Issigonis cast his eye on the lucrative military market which was being dominated by the Land Rover. Greek-born Mr Issigonis – he wasn't knighted for his contribution to the motor industry until 1969 – had joined Morris Motors back in 1936 and worked on a number of projects for the company, including the post-war Morris Minor which went into production in 1948. He took a brief break from Morris in the early 1950s, going to Alvis Cars for a while, before he was lured back to the newly-formed BMC by its chairman Sir Leonard Lord. The BMC was the largest British motor manufacturer of its day and had come into existence in 1952 through the merger of Morris Motors with the Austin Motor Company, and via the Morris connection this included the MG, Austin-Healey, Riley and Wolseley brands.

At BMC Alec Issigonis was tasked with designing a range of three cars: a large and a medium family car, plus a small town car. As a result of the fuel shortages brought about by the Suez Crisis of 1956, all efforts were focused on the smaller car initially. In 1959 this little wonder was launched as both the Austin Seven and the Morris Mini-Minor – given the established dealership networks, it was felt that marque loyalty among the car-buying public required the dual identities – although after 1962 it became universally and more famously known as the Mini. Issigonis's stroke of genius in designing the small car had been the positioning of the engine transversely, or sideways, to drive the front wheels via a unitary gearbox/drive system which shared the same engine oil as lubricant. This drastically simplified the engineering in comparison with conventional rear-drive cars while bequeathing the car its characteristically compact size. The rest is history and the Mini went on to become the best-selling British car of all time, with production exceeding the five million mark in 1986 and continuing until the year 2000.

Enter the Moke

The Moke is often regarded as a spin-off from the Mini, but it would be better described as its cousin because the two cars appear to have been conceived more or less concurrently. The Mini was aimed at the general public and the Moke at the army. Issigonis's first involvement with military vehicles had been in the 1940s with the design of the four-wheel drive

Nuffield Guppy, a light Jeep-like vehicle intended to be parachute-droppable in support of paratroop operations. However, the Second World War ended before it saw service. The Guppy is often confused with the similarly named Nuffield Gutty, for which Issigonis designed the suspension. The Gutty was a ¼ ton truck which was in production from 1951 until 1956 and it became universally known by its civilian moniker of the Austin Champ.

By the mid-1950s the British Army was expressing a need for something a little smaller, a lightweight air-portable vehicle – which the Champ definitely was not – and Issigonis saw the opportunity to apply the same design principles and many of the components used on the Mini to its military counterpart. Six minimalist prototypes were built at Longbridge and these 'Buckboards', as they were codenamed, featured the same transverse engine layout and Moulton-designed rubber suspension system as the Mini applied to a tray-like body. In terms of styling it had something of the Jeep about it with bonnet shape, flat running boards and open top, but on a smaller scale. In 1960 several Buckboards were supplied to the Army's Fighting Vehicle Research and Development Establishment (FVRDE) at Chertsey, in Surrey, for evaluation and a couple were sent to North Africa for further testing.

Unfortunately the Army was not overly impressed, especially with the vehicle's disappointingly poor ground-clearance. This led to the 1962 model, with a modified body shell featuring a hinged windscreen, a wheelbase reduced from 80 inches to 72.5 inches, plus improvements to the ground clearance which were achieved by inserting packing between the suspension and body. A metal guard sump was also added to provide protection for the 950cc engine and gear train.

When BMC published a promotional brochure for its 'front-wheel drive utility vehicle (Military Version)', it bore the name Mini Moke – 'moke' being an old slang term for a donkey or a not so good horse. The specifications provide greater detail: Engine, in-line, water-cooled, overhead-valve, four cylinder installed transversely in unit with clutch, gearbox and final drive, 948cc. Suspension, front (includes final drive) independent with levers of unequal length. Swivel axle mounted on ball joints, rubber springs and telescopic shock absorbers mounted above the top levers. Rear, independent trailing tubular levers with rubber springs and telescopic shock absorbers. Road wheels, pressed steel, 10 inch Dunlop Weathermaster tyres. 'Bodywork, pressed steel unitary construction, open-type body with vinyl-treated fabric tilt cover supported by folding tilt tubes. Front and rear wings are flat-topped to enable one vehicle to be stowed on top of another for compact transportation such as in aircraft.'

The vehicle had four detachable seats of pressed steel construction, a detachable bonnet and a windscreen that could be folded down or

The Moke's military lineage: The inspirational US Army Jeep and, *right*, the Austin Champ.

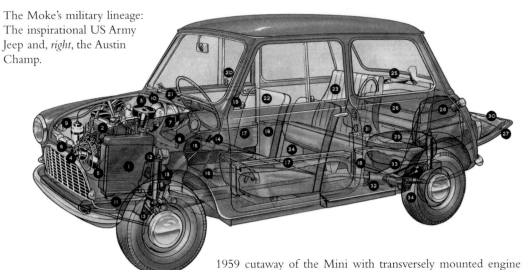

1959 cutaway of the Mini with transversely mounted engine and the rubber-springed suspension system which was shared with the Moke. *Below*, 1959 Buckboard prototype 14BT 18.

14BT 17 was a 1960 prototype used by the British Army for air-drop trials. This dramatic display at the Haynes Motor Museum in Somerset offers a unique view of the vehicle's underside. *Opposite top*: Note the semi-circular mounts for side lights and absence of side or pannier boxes. *Opposite lower*: As the front wheel moves up and down, wishbone arms hinge about the joint B compressing and pulling strut C and rubber springs D. At the rear, movement of the spring arm E is transmitted via a strut F to rubber spring G.

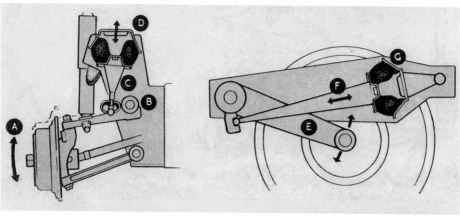

The two-engined Twini-Moke was created in 1962 as an unusual approach to four-wheel drive. The second engine of 848cc was mounted at the rear, as shown *below*, to create what in effect was the first eight-cylinder Austin. Although this solution was impractical, its excellent performance demonstrated the potential of a 4X4 Moke.

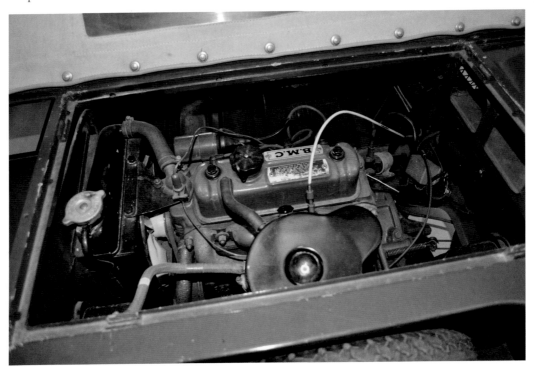

The rear engine on the Twini–Moke not only reduced the number of seats to two but also required an extra gear stick, as can be seen in this preserved example displayed at the Heritage Motor Centre in Gaydon, Warwickshire.

removed completely. The accompanying illustration of the Mini Moke (Military Version) showed the headlamps positioned on the wheel arches and a larger one-piece radiator grill of wire mesh. Instead of open triangular sills as on the Buckboard, the familiar side or pannier boxes had made an appearance, their square girder-like structure providing greater torsional stiffness and a better location for the fuel tank which had previously occupied a space behind the rear seats.

The schizophrenic Moke

Off-road the Moke proved to be surprisingly agile in most conditions thanks to its front-wheel drive, with the weight of the engine placed directly above the drive wheels. The publicity material attempted to negate the obvious lack of four-wheel drive by showing four soldiers riding in the Moke and then physically picking it up and moving it when it got stuck, but it wasn't enough to win the Army's approval. The little Moke simply couldn't compete with the larger Land Rover. Undeterred, Issigonis came up with a radical fix. In 1962 a four-wheel drive version was created by installing a second engine at the back of the vehicle, with the rear wheels remaining in the ahead position. (Issigonis had considered a separate rear steering wheel but concluded that this would 'require very superb help from an assistant'.) The loss of space given over to this extra

BMC brochure for the military version of the Mini Moke, one of the earliest uses of the name. It features the side boxes plus a large wire mesh grille with the headlamps embedded within the front mudguards.

engine inevitably limited the vehicle to two occupants. The engines had a common clutch and linked throttles, but the gear levers were separate. On the first model the extra one was on the right of the driver, in effect requiring a two-handed gear change. It was later relocated between the front seats, behind the main gear stick, and the two were linked by a coupling. This configuration can be seen on the surviving example displayed at the Heritage Motor Centre in Gaydon, Warwickshire.

It wasn't a true 4X4 with power distributed among the four wheels, and if one pair of the Twini's wheels came off the ground there was a risk of over-speeding the unloaded engine. In normal driving conditions either engine could be cut, or left in neutral, to conserve fuel. Certainly the practicalities and engineering niceties of managing the double engines could be overcome, and the eight-cylinder 1696cc Twini-Moke turned out to be a real workhorse, demonstrating outstanding off-road capabilities. An *Autocar* review, published in February 1963, enthusiastically highlighted its potential.

> When one has experienced the Double Moke's acceleration, it is breath-taking just to imagine what a Mini saloon could do in competition with a really hot engine at each end, a power-weight ratio of over 200 bhp per ton and four-wheel drive...

14

During the harsh winter of 1962/3, BMC contrived to generate considerable press coverage for the Twini when it was demonstrated battling through the snow with a small snow plough at the front and carrying a load of hay perched above the rear engine. The American Army did express some interest in the Twini and one example equipped with 12 inch wheels was sent for testing at the Tank-Automotive Command in Warren, Michigan, along with a conventional two-wheel drive model. Alas, as with the British before them, the Americans didn't come through with any orders. Only the Royal Navy took a limited interest in the Buckboard design for use on its aircraft carrier decks, although even they preferred the Citroen 2CV pick-up in this role.

Having had the Moke rejected by the military on both sides of the Atlantic, BMC resumed development of an 80 inch wheelbase model which became the pilot for a civilian version of the car. However, Issigonis didn't give up on the 4X4 theme and he later went on to design the Austin Ant. In prototype form at least, the Ant bore a close family resemblance to the Moke and, although a little bigger, it is generally considered to be its successor. When BMC became a part of the British Leyland group, the Ant project was cancelled as it would have been in direct competition with the Land Rover.

Generally considered to be the successor to the Moke, the Austin Ant was a short-lived attempt to muscle in on the military market. It was cancelled in 1968 when BMC became part of the British Leyland group.

British Mokes 1963–1968

Arrival

The civilian version of the Mini-Moke first rolled off the Longbridge production line in January 1964, the initial batch of ten destined for Papua New Guinea and Singapore. It was launched onto the British market later that same year and was available as either an Austin or Morris Moke depending on the dealership where you bought it. BMC designated the Austin Moke as the A/AB1 while the Morris version was M/AB1.

The car's design had been finalised through a number of pre-production prototypes and the new Moke closely resembled the military version in most respects, albeit with an 80 inch wheelbase giving an overall length of 10ft. As before, it had a pressed-steel open body, with sub-frames, detachable from the body, providing mounting at the front for the power pack and front wheel drive assembly incorporating the transverse engine, clutch, gearbox and differential, all of which occupied only 18 inches of space. The BMC 'A' series 850cc engine provided the power and this produced 34 bhp at 5,000 rpm and maximum torque of 44 lb ft at 2,900 rpm. It was more than enough for the lightweight car and the fuel economy was acceptable if not exceptional. Acceleration from a standing start was not up to much, with 1–60 mph taking a tawdry twenty-four seconds, or so.

At the front there had been some cosmetic changes to the face of the car, with the headlamps moved to either side of a slatted grille, Jeep-style. The bonnet, one of the few curved panels to be found on the body, was held in place by rubber catches at the front and was removable for access to the engine compartment. Along either side of the Moke's monocoque body the previously blank side boxes were now broken up by three panels providing access to the battery plus storage space for a car jack and so on. The 6.25 gallon fuel tank had been moved from the back to within the left-hand box and a wide filler cap permitted visual inspection of fuel levels, thus justifying the absence of a fuel gauge.

The Moke's interior was uncompromisingly Spartan and for your hard-earned cash, £335 of it, you got one driver's seat – metal, with press-stud attachments for cushions – and a solitary spindly windscreen wiper which needed to be started and parked manually. A central instrument panel housed speedometer, mileage recorder, warning lights for ignition, oil pressure, dirty oil filter and headlamp high-beam, plus the choke and light switches. The dip switch for the headlamps was foot operated. Overhead, the occupants were protected from the elements by a simple vinyl-treated fabric hood supported by detachable folding metal tubes. And that was it. Anything else, including such niceties as front or back

MORRIS mini-MOKE

rugged run·about with a thousand uses

BMC brochure for the civilian version of the Morris Mini–Moke from 1964. Apart from the red colour, it was identical to the Austin brochure.

passenger seats (£8 9s and £16 18s respectively), or side screens (another £30 for those) and passenger grab handles were classed as extras which the customer had to fit themselves. As for the colour range; to paraphrase Henry Ford, you could have it in any colour you wanted as long as it was Spruce Green.

'That preposterous Mini Moke'

Clearly the Moke was uncompromisingly a utility vehicle and BMC's marketing material concentrated solely on the commercial applications under the slogan, 'Rugged run-about with a thousand uses.' The first brochures – printed in black and white with red for the Morris version and green for the Austin one – tentatively listed just a few:

Hotel beach-wagon
Holiday camp taxi
Golf course caddy truck
Works transportation for manager or maintenance men
VIP factory tours
Point-to-point transport for works personnel
Site survey vehicle
Nimble work-horse for farmers, estate managers, vets

Many of these applications were perfectly valid of course, but you got the impression that the copy-writers weren't quite sure where the Moke would fit in. It had to be good for something. The brochure was illustrated with a picture of men in hard hats working on a dam, but there weren't too many of those being built. The accompanying text identified the Moke's strongest selling points as fantastic economy, front-wheel pulling power, superb road holding and sheer reliability.

Never was a vehicle so versatile and so economical as the Mini-Moke. Based on the world-proven Mini-Saloon, it's built rugged all through for sheer reliability. Cheerfully tackling any task, the Mini-Moke brings the verve of high performance to work-a-day routine. You can think of a use for the Mini-Moke.

It made no mention of the car's potential as a family or fun car. That would come later, and the company's focus on commercial usage was vital if the Moke was to escape the dreaded Purchase Tax which was applied by the Treasury to all passenger cars.

Inevitably, the newly launched, utilitarian Moke received mixed reviews from the motoring press. One journalist referred to it as

British Mokes were powered by the Austin A unit – 848cc and with maximum bhp of 34 at 5,500 rpm – an in-line water-cooled four-cylinder unit with the clutch, gearbox and final drive contained within the sump. As with the Mini, it was mounted transversely with the radiator on the left-hand side. Note how the bonnet is removable to provide access.

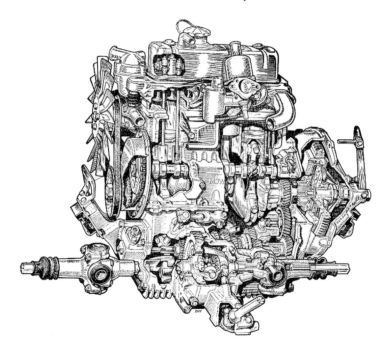

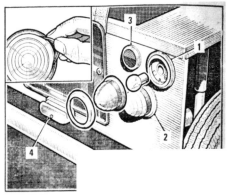 

The original rear light cluster which lacks a reversing light.

Left: Rear suspension featured independent trailing tubular levers with rubber springs and telescopic shock absorbers.

Only 18 inches of the Moke's total length are taken up by the engine, clutch, differential and transmission. Simple rubber catches hold the bonnet in the closed position.

Headlamp and side lights detail. On these early Mokes, the grille was an integral part of the front panel pressing.

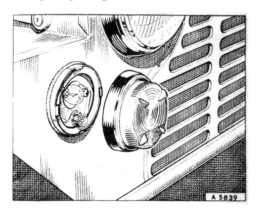

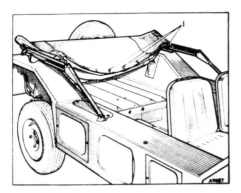

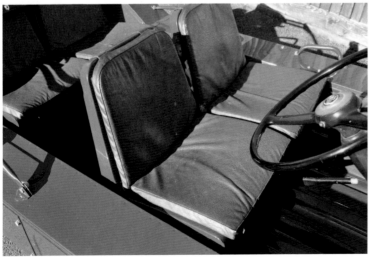

Supported on thin metal tubes, the vinyl-treated tilt, or hood, can be raised or lowered in a couple of minutes. However, it offered only minimal protection against the British weather and side screens were offered as yet another extra item. Customers only got the minimalistic pressed-steel driver's seat as standard.

1964 Austin Moke with hood in down and up positions.

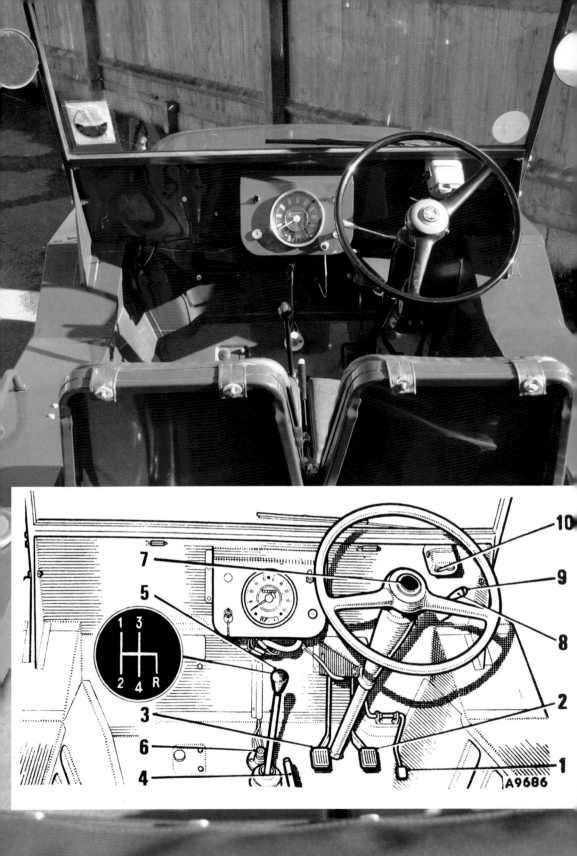

A9686

Utilitarian motoring at its best. Interior view showing the controls, listed in the Driver's Handbook as: 1) Accelerator, B) Brake, 3) Clutch, 4) Hand brake, 5) Gear lever, 6) Headlamp dip switch, 7) Horn, 8) Indicators, 9) Indicator warning light, and 10) Wiper Control to the right of the steering wheel for the single wiper, which was started and parked manually.

The instrument panel has 1) Ignition, 2) Speedometer, 3) Oil pressure warning, 4) Fuel level gauge, 5) Ignition warning light, 6) Choke, 7) Lighting switch, 8) Distance recorder and 9) Headlamp main beam light.

Note that in the car shown in these photographs the indicator stalk has been moved to a non-standard position to the left of the steering wheel.

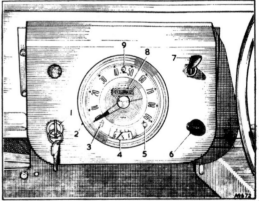

that 'preposterous Mini Moke', but staff writers on Austin's *Payload* magazine, a publication produced by the company's commercial division, adhered to the official line:

> With front-wheel drive and the power unit mounted transversely over the front wheels, maximum traction is assured over difficult terrain, circumstances to which the Moke is ideally suited. One of the great advantages of this sturdy vehicle which helps to increase its usefulness is the ease with which passengers and goods can enter or leave... There can be little doubt that the Moke is an unusual vehicle with an almost unlimited potential in the commercial world. Tough over the rough and speedy on the road, the Moke has a standard of performance and fine weather comfort belied by its stark, purposeful but oddly attractive appearance.

Oddly attractive appearance? It wasn't going to win any beauty competitions in a hurry. Other, less biased journalists who tested the car were less forgiving of its openness. Occupants sitting with their bottoms level with the side boxes felt exposed, with the road whizzing past barely a couple of feet away, and some unkind wits likened the Moke to an overgrown shopping basket.

Nonetheless its solid, sure handling did come in for praise, one journalist observing that the cornering was superb and the rubber suspension kept the car flat with little lean. Even so, the more astute commentators homed in on the Moke's vital flaws and *Which Motoring* was typical with its uncompromising assessment:

In the publicity material the Moke was regularly depicted on the golfcourse, either as an over-grown caddy or because it represented the outdoor lifestyle. The car in the colour image, *above*, is left-hand drive and this photograph may have been produced for the American marketing. (*Campbell McCutcheon*)

The primitive-looking seats, though small, were just about adequate... The hood made so much noise it was almost certainly the noisiest vehicle we have ever driven... You have to accept that the Moke is not a car for long journeys. Once you have accepted that, the Moke is fine if it is fine, and not if it's not... Unless you are very optimistic about the weather, it does seem slightly eccentric to pay nearly as much as for a Mini for a car which gives you such an unpleasant time in bad weather.

The lack of protection from bad weather conditions would crop up all too frequently. This is what Alex Markovich reported in *Popular Mechanics*:

No side windows. No doors. You just sit there, perched on the brink of disaster, your knees scrunched up because the seat doesn't adjust. The tiny 34 hp chugger takes twenty-four long seconds to reach 60 mph. The drive train is noisy. The ride is harsh. And then (the horror, the horror) it begins to rain, and passing cars get you all wet and everyone seems to be laughing at you even more than usual.

Despite the drawbacks, the Moke attracted a steady stream of commercial customers. Newspaper cuttings from the era show some of them displaying their new vehicles and they include the Devon Fire Brigade, the police patrolling Dartmoor, Wimpey Construction, and even BEA, who used the Moke as airport transport for maintenance crew. As part of a promotional campaign, the BMC Parade Team was created

Suddenly the Moke was the fashionable vehicle for record covers, including offerings from the Spencer Davis Group, the *Captain Scarlet*-inspired Spectrum and Dave Dee, Dozy, Beaky, Mick & Tich among others.

to display a string of ten Mokes at public events such as the racing at Silverstone and the Lord Mayor's parade through the City of London. They were also deployed at golf tournaments as mobile film units and transports, and their other film work is described later – *see page 79.*

A range of non-factory items extended the Moke's commercial usefulness, not to mention its weather-proofing. The Barton company in Plymouth offered an extensive selection of fibreglass hardtops, plus other accessories. *See Specials – page 67.*

All of this was very worthy, but the stuffy management at BMC failed to appreciate that the Moke's greatest appeal lay elsewhere.

Sixties chic

Despite the inevitable soakings and the thrumming of the canvas hood, two recurring themes began to emerge in the press. The Moke was very manoeuvrable and it was, to use the 'F' word again, great fun to drive. Even Markovich, who had written so disparagingly in *Popular Mechanics*, had to confess that he enjoyed the car perhaps more than any other he had driven: 'One thing it is definitely good for is fun.' More than that, the Moke also had acquired street cred. The ugly duckling, originally intended as a military mud-slugger, was still ugly but it was also very cool. Its very quirkiness and non-conformity fitting perfectly with the fashionable set and the rebellious spirit of the times, as epitomised by Traffic in the lyrics of 'Berkshire Poppies':

> He's thinking that work is all a big joke,
> While he looks in the gutter for something to smoke,
> Two hundred kids in one red Mini Moke,
> Scream down the street fully loaded.

Suddenly the Moke was everywhere. It was the vehicle of choice for album cover shoots with a procession of bands such as The Spencer

Davis Group, Spectrum and Dave Dee Dozy Beaky Mick and Tich, all spilling out of them. George Harrison owned one – his girlfriend Pattie Boyd famously posed for the paparazzi in it on the same day that The Beatles were receiving their MBEs from the Queen in 1965. Paul McCartney drove one and Brigitte Bardot appeared on and off screen in them and was famously photographed taking her dogs for a spin.

1967 proved to be a particularly momentous year for the Mini Moke. BMC unveiled the Mark II, which featured, luxury of luxuries, an additional windscreen wiper for the passenger side as well as the repositioning of horn and headlight controls onto an indicator stalk. The new Mokes were also available in Snowberry White in addition to Spruce Green. In September 1967 a bunch of white Mokes (MkI 1s as it happens) made their début in *The Prisoner* television series. Starring and co-created by Patrick McGoohan, *The Prisoner*'s stylish production and unusual allegorical story-telling was compulsive viewing and the ground-breaking series has cult status among a legion of loyal fans. These Moke taxis were the only vehicles in the mysterious Village and, dressed up with garish holiday-camp awnings and the enigmatic penny farthing logo on their bonnets, their appearance dramatically boosted public interest and awareness of the car. Mokes also cropped up in a number of other television shows, including *The Avengers*, and made a long list of feature film appearances include repeated cameos in the Bond franchise – *see Taxi for Number Six on page 79.*

A classic Sixties promotional photo featuring sunshine and girls. But what must have been the cameraman's instructions as they pensively perched on the Austin Moke?

The third event of 1967 was not nearly so welcome. The Treasury changed its mind regarding the Moke's status, deciding that it was indeed a car and accordingly would be subject to Purchase Tax. This added another £78 to the pre-tax price of £335 for the basic model. By the time you added the optional but frankly essential extras – front and rear passenger seats, heater, side screens, grab handles, sump guard and Dunlop Weathermaster tyres – the price was nudging the £500 mark. Just a whisker shy of an ordinary Mini. This badly dented the home sales. The Moke was no longer a cheap runabout – it had become a lifestyle statement, a fashion accessory, and as such it no longer made economical sense. The British climate didn't help matters either. Over the four year period from 1964 to 1968, 14,518 Mokes were produced in the UK and more than 90 per cent were exported to customers overseas. From 1966 BMC had also been making Mokes in Australia on a small scale, but elsewhere the US market looked under threat as the Moke, as built, would not meet the more stringent safety legislation about to be introduced there. When BMC became part of the British Leyland Motor Corporation, UK production of the Mini Moke was halted in 1968.

The Household Cavalry, mini-skirts, a bowler-hatted gent and a Moke – you can almost hear the chimes of Big Ben in this BOAC poster.

1969, and these thoroughly British holidaymakers, *below*, pose in their thoroughly British shorts beside a Snowberry White 'Mark II' hire car at Curaçao in the Caribbean.

Engine:

In-line, water-cooled, overhead-valve four cylinder. In unit with clutch, gearbox and final drive. Installed transversely. 848cc capacity. Compression ratio 8.3 : 1. Max bhp 34 at 5,500 rpm. Max torque 44 lb ft at 2,900 rpm.

Fuel system:

Single carburettor. Electrical fuel pump. Petrol tank capacity 6.25 gallons (28 litres).

Transmission:

Four-speed manual. Gearbox in unit with engine and final drive casing. Drive to front wheels.

Steering:

Rack and pinion.

Suspension:

Front is independent with levers of unequal length. Swivel axle mounted on ball joints. Rubber springs and shock absorbers mounted above top levers. Rear is independent trailing tubular levers with rubber springs and telescopic shock absorbers.

Brakes:

Hydraulically operated drum brakes.

Road wheels:

10 inch four-ply tubeless tyres or, for cross-country, Dunlop Weathermaster tyres with tubes.

Instruments:

Centrally mounted panel includes speedometer with petrol gauge, plus warning lights to show dynamo not charging, headlamp high-beam position (changed via a foot operated dip switch), low oil pressure and dirty oil filter element.

Bodywork:

Pressed-steel unitary construction, open-body with vinyl-treated fabric tilt cover. Fabricated pressed-steel sub-frames, detachable from body, provide mounting for engine/drive system and trailing arm suspension elements at the rear. Detachable seat of pressed-steel construction. Hinged bonnet detachable. Windscreen can be folded down or removed. Straight tubular steel bumpers. (Useful as handles when you had to lift the car!)

Dimensions and data:

Wheelbase 80 inches. Length overall 120 inches. Width overall 51.5 inches. Ground clearance 6.12 inches. Dry weight approx 10.5 cwt.

Optional extras:

Sump protector, Dunlop Weathermaster tyres, front and rear grab handles, laminated windscreen, passenger seat, two rear seats.

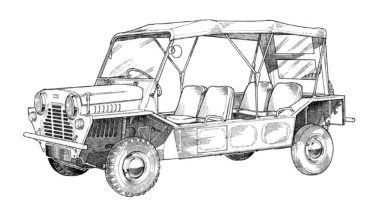

This fine Morris Moke owned by Phil Bowring is one of the so-called Mark II models, with a second windscreen wiper for the passenger and the Snowberry White finish. It also sports additional natty and very patriotic artwork on the front.

Beneath the Union Jack there lurks a very tidy engine bay. Note the Morris badge on the engine and the position of the radiator on the far right of the picture.

Australian Mokes 1966–1982

The challenge: design and produce an all-purpose vehicle with the Australian man on the land primarily in view. It must be tough and rugged. It must be capable of carrying men or materials without fuss. It must be capable of travelling where there are no tracks. It must be economical in use, simple to service. The Mini Moke is BMC's answer.

To hell with fun – the advertising copy was a mission statement of where the vehicle was to be positioned within the Australian market. To back up the message, the brochures depicted a number of 'Australian countrymen' – farmers, bridge-builders, surveyors, hunters, but mostly farmers – and a text that conjured up the vast open spaces of the Outback and the 'tough and challenging environment of national development projects'. In the make-believe world of advertising, the vehicle's shortcomings were spun as positive attributes.

Of course very special four-wheel drive vehicles can conquer the toughest going but their cost often makes them an uneconomic proposition. What is needed is a vehicle that can offer a car's low initial cost and economy of use combined with rugged power to handle rough going. Add a load carrying capacity, ease of getting in and out of the vehicle (every man on the land with gate opening and shutting problems will appreciate this!) and you have... THE MOKE!

In truth, the little Moke looked out of its depth in those vast open spaces. Assembly of the Australian Moke had commenced at a BMC

'Good on yer cobber, I'm glad to see that those pommies resisted stereotyping us Aussies as a bunch of sheep farmers.' BMC's brochure for the big-wheeled Moke.

THE
NEW
BIG
WHEEL
BMC
MOKE

BMC went to great pains to promote the Australian-built, bigger-wheeled Moke as an all-purpose vehicle for rural work, everything from carrying fodder or livestock to serving the needs of the mining industry. It was only later that it was also marketed as a recreational vehicle.

plant in Sydney in 1966, with production running in parallel with the Brits initially, but Australia became the sole manufacturing site once UK production ceased in 1968. Initially the Aussie cars were built to exactly the same spec as the British models and were marketed as the BMC Morris Mini Moke. A number of improvements were soon introduced to deal with the more demanding driving conditions down under and, with time, to meet changes in the safety and anti-pollution legislation, including those of various export destinations. These Aussiefied vehicles are sometimes described as Mark II Mokes and the most obvious external change was an increase in wheel diameter from the Mini's modest 10 inches to a more robust 13 inches. In the process the bigger wheels upped the ground clearance to 8.25 inches, but also necessitated a slight increase in vehicle width plus a wheelbase stretch from 80 inches to 82.5 inches. In addition, the rear mudguard was given a kick-back to clear the bigger wheel, the electrics cabling, brake and fuel pipes were all moved higher where they would be less susceptible to damage over rough terrain, and a sump guard was fitted as standard.

Put together, these changes gave the Moke a far more businesslike stance. It looked fit for purpose with the larger wheels now filling the wheel arches. (In comparison, all previous models with the smaller wheels suddenly looked ludicrously inadequate.) The only downside was that the larger diameter wheels resulted in an increased turning circle of 36 ft.

Big wheels and an 8 inch ground clearance make the Moke an ideal vehicle for rural work.

The versatile Moke
It will do anything you want it to do.

Over 26,000 Mokes were built in Australia and consequently the highest concentration of survivors is to be found down-under. *Above*, a 1,275cc Moke in metallic blue, built in 1981. (*Katherine Tompkins*) *Below*, an unbelievably bright green Moke photographed at a car show in Victoria. (*Sicnag*)

The Australian Army took an interest in the home-grown Moke and ordered over 200 of the big-wheelers. (*Alfvan Beem*)

There were also changes beneath that snub-nosed bonnet. Instead of the 998cc engine, a locally manufactured 1,098cc unit was introduced and an even heftier 1,275cc engine was offered as an option. However, by 1976 new anti-pollution legislation saw the 1,098cc engine replaced by an imported 988cc motor, a detoxed unit developed in the UK with an air pump and exhaust gas recirculation. This was considered by many to be a retrograde step in terms of the car's performance.

The newer models also featured a strengthened body. The solid metal seats were replaced with tubular-framed deckchair-style seating, and there were luxurious parcel shelves either side of the instrument panel. Front and rear bumpers were still just steel poles, but they were extended outwards for greater protection and the bumper supports designed to collapse before damage to the front frame or body structure could occur. The circular sidelights gave way to more modern rectangular ones. Protective quarterlights were added to the sides of the windscreen, and together with plastic mudguards these helped to keep out the dust and dirt.

The Oz Moke was still very basic, but the revised and beefier model proved to be very popular. This review comes from the March 1970 edition of *Australian Motor Sports*:

> It is taken for granted as a fun machine, but unlike many such vehicles, you don't begin to tire of the Moke after a couple of hours behind the wheel. Certainly it is far more suited to warm weather, but it is, with the optional side curtains and quarter panels entirely practical for winter motoring as long as you could fit a heater. The

Images for a later brochure showing that the Moke was suited to more than just sheep farming. It could also be used as a delivery vehicle, or in recreational mode for shopping or surfing. *Below*, pretty in red this Moke is sporting an unconventional front bumper – it looks like a piece of plastic piping. (*Steve Baker*)

longer wheelbase is a much better ride than the normal Mini, the seats are very comfortable and resemble those fitted to the Citroen 2CV and the initial Renault R4s... Australia is now the only country in the world producing the Moke and production this year will be trebled to meet the increased export demand.

The big-wheeled Moke was also making inroads into the military market. Unlike their UK counterparts, the Australian Army took an interest and after testing several Mokes, including a twelve-month stint at the Tropical Trials Establishment, they ordered over 200 of the vehicles. Other military customers included the Royal Australian Air Force and Navy, and the New Zealand Navy.

The Californian

In 1972 Leyland Australia produced a 'special export' variant commonly referred to as the Californian with obvious American intent. This was equipped with the 1,275cc engine, side marker lights and the revised rear lights included a reversing light to conform to US standards. A new fuel tank, taken from the Austin Sprite or MG Midget, was fitted beneath the rear load area in place of the original tank located in the pannier side box. The car had new seats and in keeping with its American target audience, the vinyl hood was dressed up in 'flower power' colours; black and white tiger stripes or a pattern known as Orange Bali. To cater for the export market, right or left-hand drive, imperial or metric speedometers, rear seat belts, laminated windscreen, headlamp guards and yellow headlamps (left-hand drive only) were all on the menu. In the event, these super-Mokes were barred from the USA by tougher legislation, although they were keenly scooped up by Australian enthusiasts and some made it to the UK.

Up close and personal with Peter James's Australian Moke. Behind the Leyland badge there is a 1,275cc engine with supercharger. In the rear view the filler cap is on the left-hand side box, and at the back the spare wheel is also on the left. Passengers are greeted with a notice saying, 'Get in, sit down, hold tight.'

The customised blue and orange colour scheme is based on that of the Gulf motorsport team. You don't have to have a sense of humour to own a Moke, but it does help. You can see in this photo that the grille is attached to the front rather than the earlier one-piece pressings.

It's not only the colour scheme that has been customised, with additional instrument gauges on this extended fascia. Note the distinctive kick-back on the rear mudguards, a necessity to clear the bigger wheels.

Then, in 1979 Leyland revived the Californian name to create an-upmarket sporty model to be offered alongside the standard Moke with the intention of stemming the tide of small 4X4s coming from Japan. And while it didn't have four-wheel drive, not yet at least, it did have some natty denim seats:

Denim never looked so good. The new Moke Californian, equipped with denim look hood, curtains and deluxe seats and a list of accessories to make it big news on the roads this year. Bull bars front and rear, a sport steering wheel, front and rear floor mats, spoked wheels, radial winter tread tyres, dual horns, locking spare wheel nut, chrome wheel nuts and centre caps, zip opening rear hood panel, square mirrors placed externally. Metallic paint available as an optional extra. And to top it all – no big bills to spoil your fun in the sun... Moke Californian. Get your denim seat into ours.

The Californian came in a range of bright colours, with the name displayed prominently on the side of the bonnet. What it vitally needed was some essential safety gear, such as a roll-bar, and the lap seatbelts in the back were little better than useless. Even so, the Californians enjoyed some success both within Australia and overseas, with exports reportedly going to more than sixty countries. Some found their way to the UK, specially imported by Runamoke in Battersea.

Despite the Californian facelift, the Moke was gradually losing some of its shine. In 1978 a five page article published in *Bushdriver* recited a litany of problems, from reliability and petty build-quality issues to its poor value for money. Incremental modifications had resulted in niggling faults. For example, it was impossible to unbutton the lower rear edge of the hood

Denim never looked so good. The new Moke Californian, equipped with denim look hood, curtains and deluxe seats and a list of accessories to make it big news on the roads this year.

Bull bars front and rear, a sports steering wheel, front and rear floor mats, spoked wheels, radial winter tread tyres, dual horns, locking spare wheel nut, chrome wheel nuts and centre caps, zip opening rear hood panel, square mirrors paired externally. Metallic paint available as an optional extra. And to top it all – no big bills to spoil your fun in the sun. Moke gives you up to 42 mpg, it's in the cheapest insurance category with most insurance companies and if in your excitement you knock a panel or two, it won't cost a fortune to repair. **Moke Californian. Get your denim seat into ours.**

The 1977 advertisement for the newly-launched Californian model promises fun in the sun and friends in blue denim, albeit somewhat blurry friends. The car in the advert appears to have no rear seats, which explains why his friends are perched on the sides. *Below*, a red Californian on Magnetic Island, minus the spare wheel which is normally mounted centrally at the back. (*Rene Wachter*)

Californian in dark blue with hood rolled down to reveal some sporty mods within. This vehicle has been fitted with modern low-profile tyres. A standard steel wheel is shown *left*.

Below: The hood secured in the down position, plus diagrams from the manual. The side curtains on the Australian cars were a marked improvement on earlier models.

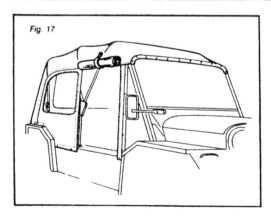

Fig. 17

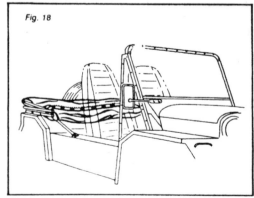

Fig. 18

without removing the spare wheel. People still wanted to like the Moke, in fact *Bushdriver* admitted that they liked it personally for some very good reasons, but added, 'We wouldn't like to have to buy one.'

The Australians had built 26,142 Mokes by the time production ceased over there in 1982. Ironically, a couple of entirely new models were in the pipeline. One was a really useful 4X4 version which had been developed in prototype form – with a single front-mounted engine instead of the Twini's ungainly twosome. The designers had also prepared preliminary visualisations for a rear-engined sports car, tentatively called the MG, which had a fibreglass shell that would sit on the Moke platform. But time, automotive fashion and the balance sheet were all against the little Moke and the production lines were turned over to the more profitable assembly of Peugeot 505s.

The Leyland Moke Pick-up

From 1975 Leyland in Australia also offered a pick-up version of the Moke. Prior to this, these had appeared only as adaptations to standard Mokes and had been offered in the UK by specialist accessory companies (such as Barton, in Devon, and also Bradburn & Wedge, of Wolverhampton, who produced the Mini-Tuk). In New South Wales Moke enthusiasts Joe and Barry Luff had made their own pick-up conversion and this caught the eye of Leyland's design team. The resulting Leyland Moke Pick-up benefited from the improvements already made to the standard Australian Mokes – bigger wheels, larger engine and improved ground-clearance. The Pick-up had a two-seater cab with a canvas cover and roll-up side panels, and at the back a 55 x 59 inch flatbed fitted with drop-sides. As this protruded over the rear of the vehicle, the spare wheel was stowed behind the cab. According to the company's promotional material, the Moke Pick-up had a multitude of applications: 'It's ideal for general farm work. Mining, surveying, pick up and delivery. You name it, Moke Pick-up can handle it.'

The Leyland general purpose Pick-up, offered from 1975, was a standard Moke with a two-seater canvas-topped cab and rear flat-bed with drop-sides.

Proving that they could put the fun back into motoring, two Aussie Californians. Above, the perfect holiday car in the bright sunshine of Magnetic Island. (*Rene Wachter*) *Below*, sunshine yellow at a car show in Victoria. (*Sicnag*)

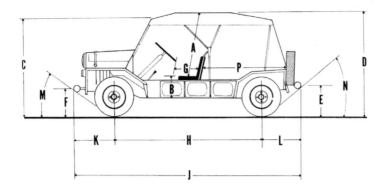

Specification Australian big wheel Moke

Engine:

In-line, water-cooled, overhead-valve four cylinder. In unit with clutch, gearbox and final drive. Installed transversely. 998cc capacity. Compression ratio 8.3:1. Max bhp 40 at 5,250 rpm. Max torque 52 lb ft at 2,700 rpm.

Fuel system:

Single carburettor. Electrical fuel pump. Petrol tank capacity 6.25 gallons.

Transmission:

Four-speed manual. Gearbox in unit with engine and final drive casing. Drive to front wheels.

Steering:

Rack and pinion.

Suspension:

Front is independent with levers of unequal length. Swivel axle mounted on ball joints. Rubber springs and shock absorbers mounted above top levers. Rear is independent trailing tubular levers with rubber springs and telescopic shock absorbers.

Brakes:

Hydraulically operated drum brakes.

Road wheels:

Pressed steel with 13 inch Dunlop Weathermaster tyres with tubes.

Instruments:

Centrally mounted panel includes speedometer with petrol gauge, plus warning lights.

Bodywork:

Rotodipped pressed-steel unitary construction, open-body with vinyl-treated fabric tilt cover. Fabricated pressed-steel sub-frames, detachable from body, provide mounting for engine/drive system and trailing arm suspension elements at the rear. Sheet steel sump protector attached to sub-frame. Two tubular seats made of polythene foam over canvas base covered with PVC coated leather cloth. Hinged bonnet detachable. Windscreen can be folded down or removed. Straight tubular steel bumpers.

Dimensions and data:

Wheelbase 83 inches. Length overall 120 inches. Width overall 57 inches. Ground clearance 8 inches.

Specification for Moke Californian

Introduced in 1979, the Californian also had the 998cc engine and featured a number of additional items as standard: Spoked wheels, denim-look high-back seats, hood and side curtains, shaped roo bars front and back, a sport steering wheel, floor mats, locking spare wheel nut, chrome wheel nuts and centre caps and squared mirrors. Not forgetting the Californian bonnet decals. Optional extras included metallic paint, rear seats and rear seat lap belts, plus roll bars.

Portuguese Mokes 1983-1993

Many happy returns

Despite the demise of the Moke down under, the Californian had a tenacious grip on life and in 1983 production was switched to the British Leyland Portugal assembly facility at the Industria Montagem Automoveis factory in Setubal. The first cars came off the line in 1984 and interest in the Portuguese-built Californians was high. They were sold throughout the world through Austin Rover's dealership network, and although the company took the decision not to offer them via its UK showrooms, they did sell the import concession to Dutton Cars in Worthing, Sussex, a company better known for its own range of sporty component or kit cars. The Moke Californian was supplied in its complete form and the Moke's return home was well received as *Alternative Cars* reported in January 1984, albeit with the usual caveats:

> The gap of fifteen years since the last time a new Moke was seen on these shores is not apparent in its design, and although it could never be called ultra-modern or refined, it is definitely trendy. We cannot emphasise enough how much fun the Moke was and confidently predict it will become the car to be seen in during 1984.

That's if enough people were prepared to fork out the not inconsiderable £4,360 purchase price for a Californian. Admittedly this included the hood, 13 inch alloys, high-back seats, roll-cage and roo-bars, but it was actually £1,000 more than the cost of a basic Mini and a mere £300

The promotional literature for the Portuguese Moke ignores functionality – this time it was all about the fun.

Opposite page: Interior detail of a 1989 Moke and, inset, the same model in all–white version. The Moke 25 was produced as a special edition to mark the car's twenty–fifth anniversary. (*Joost J. Bakker*)

Moke 25 photographed at the 2010 Mini gathering, held at the Motoring Heritage Centre in Gaydon. *Below*, red Moke with non–standard wheels at the Schaffen Fly and Drive event in the Netherlands, 2012. (*Ad Meskens*)

Reminiscent of the 1960s promotional photo on page 31, this time a Portuguese Moke on the harbour at St Tropez, clearly showing the tent-like zip-up doors. (*FaceMePLS*)

away from the 4X4 Suzuki SJ410. The trouble was that many non-standard components had crept in to the Aussie Moke. Those 13 inch wheels, for example, made for a good Moke, but they required special trailing arms for the rear suspension, not to mention the forming of the kick-back to the rear mudguard. Apart from the wheels there was the differential, which had a ratio particular to the Moke. They sound like little details but they soon added up.

Meanwhile, parent company Austin Rover, as Leyland in the UK had become known, remained supportive of the Portuguese operation and wanted to hang on to the Moke because it provided extra quota for their products. Accordingly, they despatched a recently-retired automotive consultant named Jim Lambert off to Portugal to get things sorted out. He would later admit that when he got there things were even worse than he had anticipated. The design, production quality, cost and finances were in a mess, and matters were further exasperated by endemic problems with labour relations. The plant was declared bankrupt in December 1984.

At that point there were thirty or forty Mokes in various stages of completion at Setubal, and a further 260 vehicles were crated up in the UK. In order to salvage the situation, and the Moke, Lambert identified an alternative assembly plant at Vendas Novas, and in the dead of night he spirited away the tooling and other gear. The remaining cars – or units in the industry parlance – both at Setubal and in the UK, were taken to the new plant and, working with newly-trained but minimal staff, Lambert saw the first Mokes roll off the line two months later. By all accounts the build quality was better than ever and, suitably encouraged, he was keen to keep the Moke in production.

The Moke 25 in detail. *Above*, note the side light on the mudguard and the reversion to round sidelights. *Below*, Austin Rover engine with radiator located on the left-hand side (nearest to camera).

Still pretty plain, the dashboard with central instrument fascia and parcel shelves to either side. The heater pipe can be seen snaking up on the left-hand side. *Below*, high-back seats, folding rear seat and centrally mounted spare wheel.

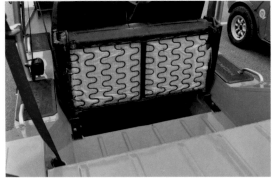

Brochure illustration for the Cagiva produced Moke. This varied only slightly from the previous Portuguese models. *Below*, a black Cagiva Moke at a car show in the UK, bearing a radiator sign for the 2011 London to Brighton Mini Run.

The Moke 86

Jim Lambert created what became known as the Moke 86. This incorporated the low-compression 998cc A-series engine, an economy-ratio gearbox, standard differential and, as a nod to the Aussies, new 12 inch diameter wheels. They might be a little smaller but they still possessed most of the advantages of the bigger wheels while requiring only standard Mini trailing arms. The slight reduction in wheel diameter also meant that the rear mudguards could return to their simpler vertical profile. Moreover, using standard and more readily available parts was vital in keeping production costs down and profitability up, which was essential if the Moke was to survive. In August 1985 the board of Austin Rover gave their go-ahead and the Lambert/Portuguese Mokes emerged from the plant in February 1986.

The revamped Moke had a far softer appearance than its predecessors. Its stance was less aggressive, more friendly, and it looked like the sort of car you probably wouldn't want to get dirty. There was the white flush wheel trim taken from the Mini, the straightened rear wheel-arch with moulded mud skirts, a repositioning of the spare wheel centrally at the rear as well as, most noticeably, new high-backed seats and a sturdy roll-cage that extended right to the back of the car. This not only provided better access to the rear seats, it was also an anchor point for rear seatbelts. Furthermore, it allowed the hood to be fixed in a choice of configurations – either fully up, half or fully rolled back, or removed completely. In addition, the rear window could be rolled up and fastened to the roll-cage for improved 'air-conditioning' on hotter days. In terms of performance, the high gearing helped to eke out the best from the little A-series engine and the disc brakes were a vast improvement.

Interviewed by *Autocar* in November 1986, Lambert described the potential market spread for the Moke 86:

> I believe it's the right vehicle for the islands of the Caribbean, for places like Portugal, for Spain, for Greece, for Malta, for the holiday market and for the rich enthusiast who can afford a Jaguar but would rather run around in a Moke.

With the possible exception of the Jag drivers, these all turned out to be good customers, but the lion's share – 90 per cent – stayed within Europe, with the majority of the cars going to France.

The Italian job

By 1990 the system of import quotas had changed sufficiently for Austin Rover to consider letting the Moke go and it was sold to the Italian

Cagiva Moke seen at a Mini Gathering in Cirencester in 2010. Externally there is little to distinguish it from earlier Portuguese Mokes, but under the bonnet it is another matter. For the first time on a Moke the radiator is positioned in front of the engine.

The lion's share of the Portuguese manufactured Mokes went to France. This example was photographed in Paris in 2011. (*Besopha*) Another blue Cagiva Moke, this time snapped on the Greek island of Kos. (*Mrs Logic*)

motorcycle makers Cagiva. Wishing to cash in on the Moke's cache, their promotional material announced that the cult car of the sixties was back and it was 'just as much fun now as it was back in those heady days in the Kings Road'.

The Italians had no rights to the Mini name and accordingly the 1,500 cars they built from 1991 until 1993 were branded simply as Mokes, and these are generally referred to as Cagiva Mokes nowadays. They were essentially the same as Lambert's Moke 86 and were even built at the same assembly plant in Vendas Novas. Cagiva made some minor changes, with refinements to the seats and hood, and for the first time on a Moke the radiator was mounted in front of the engine, behind the grill. But with costs spiralling and production output exceeding orders, Cagiva took the decision to temporarily halt production in 1993 while they transferred the tooling and equipment to their own factory in Italy. This hiatus turned out to be the end of the road for the Moke and production was not resumed.

In its various forms the Moke had been in production from 1964 until 1993, with a few breaks along the way. During that time 14,518 were manufactured in the UK, 26,142 in Australia and another 9,277 in Portugal (roughly 8,500 Californians or Moke 86s and 1,500 by Cagiva), bringing the grand total to just under 51,000 vehicles. Admittedly this is a mere drop in the ocean compared with the Mini's prodigious 5.25 million – about 0.97 per cent in fact. But that's not too shabby for the little rag-top runabout named after a donkey.

Specification for Moke 86 and Cagiva

Engine:

In-line, water-cooled, overhead-valve four cylinder. In unit with clutch, gearbox and final drive. Installed transversely. 998cc capacity. Compression ratio 8.3: 1. Max bhp 39 at 4,750 rpm. Max torque 44 lb ft at 2,900 rpm. (Radiator in front of the engine on Cagiva.)

Transmission:

Four-speed Gearbox in unit with engine and final drive casing. Drive to front wheels.

Suspension:

Front is independent with levers of unequal length. Swival axle mounted on ball joints. Rubber springs and shock absorbers mounted above top levers. Rear is independent trailing tubular levers with rubber springs and telescopic shock absorbers.

Brakes:

Disk at the front, drum at back.

Road wheels:

Pressed steel with 12 inch low profile radials.

Instruments:

Centrally mounted panel, parcel shelf to either side.

Bodywork:

Pressed-steel construction, open-body with vinyl-treated fabric tilt cover. Steel roll-cage and shaped roo bars front and rear.

Dimensions and data:

Wheelbase 80 inches. Length overall 127 inches. Width overall 56 inches.

Optional extras:

Heater, air conditioning (yes really), alloys, tinted windscreen, sump guard, rear seats, stereo, spare wheel cover, hood bag, custom trim/interior, lead-free conversion.

The Plymouth-based Barton company produced a range of Moke accessories, including hard tops. The yellow example was photographed at Drummond Castle. (*Jim Gifford*) *Left*, a Barton-topped Moke at the NEC Classic Car Show in 2012. *Below*: A Police Moke on patrol in Dartmoor.

Specials

Mokes have been adapted for a number of specialist roles and from the early days the Barton company in Devon offered a range of accessories including hard tops, either all-over or as partial cabs, plus front and rear towing brackets and assorted winches, crop spraying equipment, even breakdown/wrecker gear, a transportable lubrication unit, foamite fire fighting equipment and variations on open or closed trucks. Their catalogue even showed a mobile bookmakers' or auctioneers' rostrum.

The Moke's simple angular body has also attracted more recent customisers and their efforts have resulted in a number of six-wheelers. The Moke 6 first appeared in 1992 as a publicity vehicle for Duncan Hamilton, who was looking to become the official distributor for Cagiva Mokes in the UK. The story goes that he found himself with a good front and a good rear end from two Mokes left over after being catapulted into a concrete wall during crash testing to meet vehicle safety requirements. These were used to create the six-wheeler and in 1994 it was purchased by Tresco Estates in the Isles of Scilly, and refitted with a shed-like superstructure and painted dark green it served as an 8–10 person people carrier. It has since been sold to private owners in the UK and has been lovingly restored to its original condition.

There have been several other six-wheelers. Gerry Anderson, of *Thunderbirds* fame, used them as the basis for the SHADO jeeps in his *UFO* television series and he also had at least one as a camera platform. *See Taxi for Number Six on page 79.* And remember Doc Brown's DeLorean in the *Back to the Future* films? Its flux capacitor worked on organic rubbish and now Australian biofuel specialists Oz Future Fuels have

There's stretching and there's stretching – this fourteen seater looks highly improbable. (*Trond Bremseth*)

This Road–Rail Moke developed for Western Australia Railways had guidance wheels on retractable frames front and back.

Opposite: Six-wheel Moke 6 was originally built in 1992 as a publicity vehicle for Duncan Hamilton. (*CédEm*) And the Aussies love their big wheels. (*Moo_Mo1*)

created a stretched six-wheeler to demonstrate their real-life gasification technology. The capacity of the extra-long green Moke was needed to accommodate the bulky equipment which turns ordinary garden waste, such as lawn clippings and dead leaves, into methane fuel.

At the other extreme, the Shorty Moke or 'Schmitty' is often presented as a chopped Moke, but in fact this diminutive 92.5-inch-long car was only a lookalike. Even shorter than the Mini, or the newer Smart car for that matter, it was made for a brief period in the 1980s by Schmitt Automobiles in France.

Road-rail Mokes

In October 1967, *Railway Transportation* magazine reported that engineers from the Tasmanian Government Railways had devised a road-rail Moke as a maintenance and line-inspection vehicle. This involved fitting steel flanges behind the ordinary road wheels to keep the rubber tyres on the rails. (All-metal wheels were tried but abandoned because of their weight and the excessive vibration.) The engineers had to narrow the rear sub-assembly and reposition the front shocks to accommodate the flanged wheels. A number of these 'Mokomotives' were put to work by the railway company throughout the 1970s, and similar road-rail conversions were seen on the Central Australia Railways. An alternative system was developed for Western Australia Railways involving a Moke with small guidance railway wheels mounted on retractable frames extending at the front and rear. These could be raised or lowered by a hydraulic ram activated by the driver. In operation, the steering on the road-rail Mokes was locked in the straight-ahead position.

Ken Butterfield and his Moke during restoration. *Below*, John Walpole with the Austin Mini-Moke which was purchased in November 1964 and has remained in his family ever since.

The Joy of Moking

There is no such thing as a typical Moke owner/enthusiast, although all of them probably have a trace of exhibitionism or eccentricity tucked away deep in their DNA. Some lucky souls possess prize Mokes which have been in the family since new. John Walpole, for example, is the proud owner of a fine 1964 Austin Moke which was originally bought by his uncle, a doctor in Wales who used it to make his rounds. The car has received some attention over the years, but it remains in a beautiful and mostly original condition and John uses it to pop down to the shops or, occasionally, for more adventurous excursions. A couple of years ago he drove to Scotland and back and he has also taken the car on continental trips. Other Mokers are equally proud of their later models, whether they be big-wheeled Aussies or the Portuguese cars. Some are devout purists, preserving their vehicles faithful in as-built condition, while others seek to express their own personalities by improving engine performance or through a new paint job. More extreme Mokers want nothing more than to throw their Mokes about in a bit of mud or take them to the ends of the Earth, while the customisers want to stretch, shorten and generally pimp their cars – *as shown in the Specials section on page 67*. And some just want to be Patrick McGoohan. It really doesn't matter which camp you fall into just so long as you enjoy your Moke to the max.

Buying and restoring a Moke

So what is a Moke likely to cost nowadays? It's a bit like enquiring about the length of a piece of string. There are so many models and the choice will depend on what you want to achieve with your Moke and the girth of your wallet. Within the UK, prices are continuing to climb steadily with time and increased rarity, and some general guidelines can be drawn from recent sales. If you are hoping for a really good original sixties Moke say, with low mileage, you can expect to fork out around £15,000 or probably more like £17,000. Essex-based Moke specialists Runamoke recently (in 2013) offered a renovated 1,275cc Aussie Californian for £15,750. The Portuguese-built Mokes can be found for half that. Many of these will be left-hand drive models from Spain, Portugal or even further afield and there may be import/transport costs to consider. However, the good news is that conversion to right-hand drive is a straightforward matter.

The combination of the Moke's angular body, its simplicity of construction and the commonality of parts make it an ideal candidate for a restoration project. Rust can be the enemy, especially on earlier

The Australian owner of this Morris Mini Moke has dressed it up with some shiny chromework. (*Flying Cloud*) Many owners take part in special runs. This British-owned Cagiva has been entered in the 2011 London to Brighton Mini Run.

Moke owners like nothing better than to get together to chat about their cars.

models. It flourishes in those places where the metal has been folded or joined, and where water collects in the pannier boxes. Thankfully, the running gear and mechanicals are from the Mini and far easier to source. Body panels and parts are supplied by a number of specialist companies, although it is those awkward items such as original seats that can be harder to find and consequently very expensive. Roy Scott's *Mini Moke – A Comprehensive Guide to Restoration* is essential reading – *see Resources on page 95*. And if you don't want to tackle a full restoration yourself, there are firms that will do the donkey work for you.

Beware imitations!

As stated elsewhere, the Mini Moke is not and never was a kit-car. The confusion arises because of the suitability and availability of the Mini as a donor vehicle for self-build projects. Combined with the cult status of the Moke, this has spawned a subculture of home-built lookalikes and the term 'Moke' is frequently used in a wider generic meaning. These non-Mokes might be cheaper than the genuine article, although not necessarily, and some – whisper it quietly – are very worthy projects in their own right. Examples directly inspired by the Moke include the clone-like Andersen Mini Cub and also the Jimini, while the long list of assorted Mini-based cars includes the Scamp, the boxy and slightly futuristic Hustler, the Del Tech Nomad, the Gecko, Mule, Navajo, Yak and a veritable menagerie of others. You will sometimes spot them at Mini events sidling up to the Mokes, and the Andersen Cubs or Jimini cars in particular are frequently mistaken for Mokes by the unaware. But don't be fooled, these lookalikes are mere shadows of the real thing.

A prime candidate for restoration this neglected Moke was recently photographed in Cyprus. (*Mike Gabb*) *Below*, diagram of the Moke's body panels. In comparison with other cars there are very few curves on a Moke, as shown, making life much simpler for the restorer.

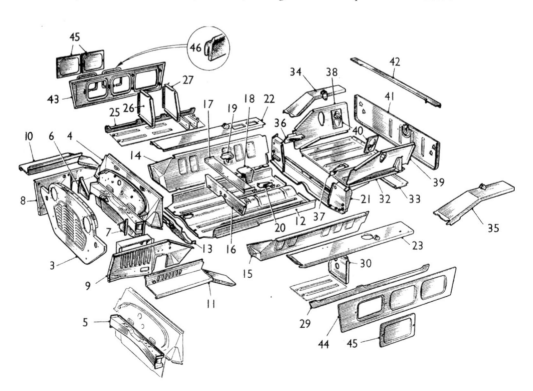

Events

Mokers like to congregate when they can. They can't help it and this is a great way to meet with fellow enthusiasts to discuss Moke matters and to socialise. These gatherings happen up and down the country, either at classic car shows – and here the Mokers have the advantage of being able to join in with most Mini-based events – or at Moke-specific events either nationally or locally. Every year, a number of Mokes take part in the annual London to Brighton Mini Run and similar runs happen in other parts of the country. Within the UK these are usually organised by the Mini Moke Club, or by regional sub-groups, and there are corresponding organisations in other parts of the world. Interest is especially strong down under, where they have two groups, the Moke Owners Association in Victoria and the South Australian Moke Club. Mokers from different countries can get together at the International Mini Moke Meeting. In 2012 this took place in the Black Forest in Germany, and the 2013 event is due to be held in Luxembourg.

Extreme Moking

Far away from the Kings Road, the Moke has turned out to be a surprisingly competitive creature and many have been entered in races and rallies as well as taking part in autocross and hill-climbing competitions.

In 1963 a double engined Twini-Moke was entered in the Targa Florio open road endurance race held in the mountains of Sicily near Palermo. Closer to home, John Player & Sons sponsored four special 1,275cc Cooper S-engined Mokes in autocross competitions in the late 1960s. John Crawford and Hans Tholstrup drove halfway around the world in an Australian-built Californian on the gruelling 1977 Singapore Airlines London to Sydney Rally. Sponsored by Coca Cola, their 1,275cc Cooper S 'Coke Moke' covered the 18,600 miles over thirty days to finish in 35th place. Apart from problems with repeatedly broken shocks and an incident in Yugoslavia with broken engine stays, the little rag-top acquitted itself well, without a single engine failure. Mokes are also to be found exploring various remote corners of the world, including the Australian outback and the far-flung Pitcairn Island. Moke enthusiasts continue to enjoy the fresh air – they don't have much choice in the matter – and regular green-laning and off-road events take place throughout the UK. So go on, get out there and get dirty.

A 1966 Austin Mini-Moke adapted for speed. The windscreen has been chopped and the chassis lowered with new wheels. The bonnet has a bulge at the back to accommodate the turbo-charger on the Rover engine.

Further modifications have been made to the interior, with a new instrument panel and racing seats. It also has a reduced-height rear roll cage. Note the additional air holes above the grille.

Portmeirion and Mokes have become inseparable ever since they appeared as Village Taxis in the cult television show *The Prisoner*. The example shown above was said to have been one of the original cars used in the filming and was displayed outside the souvenir shop until sold to an American collector. (*Francis Robinson*)

Taxi for Number Six

In the 1960s the Mini Moke's quirky styling soon caught the eye of film-makers, especially in the field of science fiction where it appeared modern, trendy, almost other-worldly. Its small size also made it well suited to film sets or locations where other vehicles might have been too big and consequently the Moke went on to have a glittering career as a star of film and television Its breakthrough performance came on 29 September 1967, when British television audiences tuned in to see the very first episode of *The Prisoner*. The driving force behind this ground-breaking series was the actor Patrick McGoohan, who had already enjoyed huge success playing the lead role of John Drake in *Danger Man*. Viewers were expecting something along similar lines, and to some degree the unnamed prisoner, labelled by his captors as Number Six, could be seen as a continuation of John Drake's story, although McGoohan would never confirm or deny that assumption. But more than that, *The Prisoner* was an entirely new television experience. The surreal game of cat and mouse set in the holiday camp-like atmosphere of the sinister Village was dreamlike, even psychedelic. Often baffling, above all else *The Prisoner* was incredibly and undeniably cool.

The show became an instant hit and the seventeen-episode series has continued to invite debate on its merits and meaning ever since. A major part of the appeal was the look of the programme, through the choice of location – Portmeirion in the north of Wales – and the use of the latest gadgetry and technology, everything from innovative cordless telephones and automatic doors to the surveillance equipment. As a free man the central character had bombed around London in a Lotus 7, but in captivity he had to make do with the Village taxis, 'local services only'. These little white cars with their deckchair-striped awnings were, of course, Mini Mokes.

Four Mokes were used in the making of the programme – at least that's how many appeared on screen at any one time – mostly as taxis, although they sometimes doubled-up as ambulances. The vehicles were specially prepared for the filming by Wood & Pickett, London, in the summer of 1966. The mods included tilting the windscreens into a more upright position, presumably to allow actors to stand while riding in the Moke (or possibly to reduce reflections), spats were added to the rear wheel arches and new candy-striped hoods fitted. These were squared off at the back. During filming the normal number plates were replaced with 'Taxi' signs, although these were omitted in one episode.

The fate of the Mokes has intrigued *Prisoner* and Moke aficionados

Not a number? Well actually... It was thought that the remaining Mokes used in the filming of *The Prisoner* had disappeared without trace, probably to be recast by the film company. That is until HLT 709C was discovered in a barn in the Netherlands. Unusually, this vehicle had appeared in one episode bearing its registration number to the camera instead of the usual Taxi plate. (*Nicholas Verhoeven*) *Above*, Portmeirion Moke. (*Francis Robinson*)

ever since. It is thought that the cars were returned to London after the shooting on location, possibly for further studio work. At least one, registration CFC 916C, was known to have survived as it was displayed outside the Village shop in Portmerion for many years before being bought by an American enthusiast. It was thought that the rest had disappeared, that is until recently when one was discovered in a barn in the Netherlands. This is HLT 709C – the registration appeared on-screen in the 'Living in Harmony' episode – and it is currently awaiting restoration by its new owner.

Mokes also turned up in a handful of other TV shows from the same era, including *The Saint, The Persuaders, The Monkees* plus several episodes of *The Avengers*, another popular quirky British programme that owed more to surreal situations than solid story lines. And when not showing its face in front of the cameras, the Moke was often used as a camera platform because of its low and open deck. When Gerry Anderson turned to live action instead of puppetry for his *UFO* television series in 1970, he included a pair of six-wheelers dressed up as SHADO jeeps. These had actually been built the year before for his unsuccessful film release, *Doppelganger* – also known as *Journey to the Far Side of Sun* in the USA – and they were painted blue for their new role in *UFO*. Anderson adopted six-wheelers as camera platforms, and there are many other examples of standard Mokes being used in this manner.

Now pay attention 007...

When it comes to famous movie motors, we automatically think of James Bond, especially the Aston Martins and Lotuses which vied for attention at the heart of this long-running franchise. You might be able to list some of the other vehicles which played supporting roles, even the 2CV and a double-decker bus for that matter, but what about the humble Mini Moke? In fact, this gadget-free car has appeared in no less than four of the Bond blockbusters.

The first occasion was in *You Only Live Twice* (1967), Sean Connery's fifth and finest outing as 007. Here a pair of yellow Mokes were used as runabouts in Ernst Blofeld's secret base within a hollow volcano. The massive film set, complete with monorail and rocket launch gantry, was created at the Pinewood Studios and must rank as one of the greatest Bond sets of all time. In fact, it was so impressive that we never stopped to wonder how the Mokes had got from Longbridge to the villain's secret lair in Japan. On the other hand, Longbridge to Buckinghamshire makes perfect sense. *Live and Let Die* (1973) was set in the Caribbean and in one scene Bond – by this time played by Roger Moore – drives a white Moke down to the harbour. A diecast model

of this vehicle was presented as part of the James Bond Car Collection
– *see Miniature Mokes on page 86*. In *The Spy Who Loved Me* (1977) the
crew of the *Liparus* supertanker use a Moke in one short scene. And
finally, in *Moonraker* (1979) the yellow Mokes ride again – possibly
the same ones as before – popping up as transports for another rocket
launch. Bond and Dr Goodhead hide in a trailer.

Other non-Bond cinematic offerings are a mixed bag, including:
Carry on Camping (1969), *Crossplot* (1969), *12+1* (1969), *More* (1969),
Camille (1969), *Mission Monte Carlo* (1974), *Goodbye Emmanuelle*
(1977), *Gargantua* (1998) and *Ritual* (2001). One film probably best
forgotten is *Salt & Pepper* (1968), a preposterous caper starring Sammy
Davis Jr, Peter Lawford and a supposedly amphibious and bullet-proof
Moke with the registration plate SALT 1.

That's just a selection of the English language films and Mokes also
crop up in a number of foreign films, French ones in particular. But
the final cinematic salute belongs to that most iconic of British films
from the sixties, the original version of *The Italian Job* (1969), which
starred Michael Caine and a famous trio of Mini Coopers. In one of the
earlier London street scenes, shortly after Charlie Crocker is released
from prison, an eagle-eyed viewer might spot a Moke lurking in the
background. Don't blink or you will miss it.

Dinky Toys 106, the *Prisoner* Mini–Moke, has become an extremely collectable diecast. It
features the distinctive striped awning and spare wheel cover, with brown panels and running
boards plus penny–farthing logo on the bonnet. (*Stephan Hacker*)

Noakes in a Moke – the *Blue Peter* crew posed in a white Moke for the programme's 1967 annual cover. To show the presenters more clearly, the windscreen has been removed and the wipers bent down behind the fascia. *Below*: Spacey six-wheelers, built for Gerry Anderson's ill-fated film *Doppelganger*, were given a new lick of blue paint to become SHADO jeeps in the *UFO* television series. This surviving example was photographed at the now-closed Cars of the Stars museum in the Lake District. (*Ken Butterfield*)

Max. Speed	70 m.p.h. (112 km.)	
B.H.P.	34 (Ch. SAE)	
Comp. Ratio 8.3:1		
C.C.	848	

2⅞" (73 mm.)

106 'Prisoner' Mini Moke

DINKY
TOYS

No. 106, *The Prisoner* Moke, as illustrated in the Dinky catalogue. The company's plans to create a new toy were thwarted when McGoohan refused to have his face on the promotional material, and instead Dinky reused their existing mould from the 342 Austin Moke. It was also used for the military 601 Austin Paramoke, which came with its own parachute, and yet again for 350 Tiny's Moke from *The Enchanted House*. (*Stephan Hacker*)

Miniature Mokes

Without question, the appearance of the Mini Moke taxis in *The Prisoner* generated enormous interest in the car, just as it had for the Lotus 7 which Patrick McGoohan's nameless character had driven in the London scenes. However, unlike the Lotus the Moke was also immortalised in a diecast miniature and to this day, almost half a century later, the iconic Dinky car 106 continues to be an enduring must-have among toy collectors.

When *The Prisoner* was first broadcast in 1967, the concept of spin-off merchandising was still largely untapped and consequently there was little for the fans to buy. In fact, it was the Meccano company, the makers of the Dinky range, who raised the idea with the television production company in the first place. They proposed producing a totally new diecast model, complete with No. 6 figure, to be widely promoted using McGoohan's image on the packaging and supporting advertising material. Dinky had previously enjoyed unprecedented sales with its *Thunderbirds* and *Captain Scarlet* vehicles – the SPV or Spectrum Pursuit Vehicle was their best selling model by a long shot – and they were confident that there was sufficient interest in *The Prisoner*. Unfortunately, McGoohan refused to allow his face to be used to promote a toy and as Dinky had already forked out for the rights, they went ahead on a lower-key product reusing their existing Austin Moke dies. These moulds had been created for their first Austin Mokes produced in 1966; number 342 in metallic green with grey canopy, as well as 601, a khaki green military version complete with plastic platform and parachute. (No doubt much used and abused by a generation of school boys.)

Dinky's Prisoner Moke was numbered 106, a reuse of a redundant earlier model designation in line with their policy of numbering the TV cars in the low hundreds. It was launched in February 1968, coincidentally the same month as the TV series came to an end, and the modified Moke featured a white paint job with tan running boards and side panels, plus penny farthing logo on the bonnet, an aerial added on the front wheel arch, new spun aluminium wheel hubs, a white plastic canopy with red stripes together with a matching rear wheel cover. The model remained in production for four years during which the minor details of the painting, engine colour, and so on, varied to some degree. The price of the cars increased regularly during that time, going from 6s 3d up to 6s 11d (pre-decimal money), but the *Prisoner* Moke was always a shilling more than the standard model.

Surprisingly, the *Prisoner* Moke was replaced by another TV-inspired model, the number 350 Tiny's Mini Moke from *The Enchanted House*, a

Rear view of 106 *Prisoner* Mini Moke showing striped awning and the easily lost matching spare wheel cover. This has become one of the most sought after Dinky diecasts and accordingly various spares, including the wheel cover, are now available for the restorers. (*Stephan Hacker*) The Moke from the James Bond Car Collection is slightly smaller than the Dinky cars. It is fairly accurate apart from the small wheels. The actual car in *Live and Let Die* had bigger 13 inch wheels.

little-remembered children's programme which was broadcast by ITV at lunchtimes. Tiny's Moke was bright orange/red, had the same white canopy as 106 only with yellow stripes, and was distinctive for the way Tiny's head poked up through a hole. Tiny, I should explain, was a giraffe.

All of Dinky's Mokes remain highly collectible, especially the TV-related models, although ironically that blessed giraffe's car is rarer and hence more valuable than the *Prisoner* Moke. Having said that, it is not uncommon to see a 106 in reasonably good condition with its original box selling for anything between £80 and £150. Even more if it is MIB – 'mint in box' in diecast parlance – i.e. perfect and complete with the spare wheel cover. A first issue 106 with gold engine recently sold for well over £200. Replacement parts are widely available and many a battered old *Prisoner* Moke has been reborn with a lick of paint and a replica box. Tiny's gaudy Moke realises similar prices. The ordinary 342 standard Mokes are far more common – they were among the cheapest cars in the Dinky range – and can be found for just a few pounds depending on condition, although the Para-Moke with original box and bubble-packaging can easily fetch £50 or more.

Non-Dinky Mokes

Despite their current desirability, the Dinky Mokes were always intended as toys rather than models and accordingly they lacked the accuracy of later diecasts which were aimed more specifically at the adult collector. In the 1980s and 1990s the Portugese company Vitesse produced a range of around a dozen or so Moke models in 1:43 scale. Naturally, there were several Portugese Mokes in the range, including a Californian and variants of the Cagiva car, but other models were included: the 1964 British-built Moke in Spruce Green or Snowberry White, plus a 1968 Australian Moke in blue. Presented in special display boxes with mirror panels, their detailing was generally of a high standard. Started in 1982, Vitesse went into liquidation in April 2000 and the name was acquired by the Sun Star Group, which has since relaunched the brand.

There have been other Moke or Moke-inspired toys and model cars over the years. Most recently, collectors were treated to a white Moke from the film *Live and Let Die* which was issued as part of the James Bond Car Collection (issue 24) produced by Danjag. In 1:43 scale, it perpetuates Roger Moore's crimes against fashion with the tiny figure of 007 sitting at the wheel resplendent in a blue safari suit. One non-diecast model worth looking out for is the Spark 1:43 Gold Leaf Racing Team Mini Moke Lotus Transporter from 1968. Cast in resin, this fine model has a hard-top Moke pulling a Lotus 47 Europa on its trailer.

Mini's Beachcomber concept car was unveiled in 2010. Like the Moke, it has open sides and a removable canvas roof. But here the similarities end, especially as it was suggested the car would get removable body panels. Not that it matters, as the concept is unlikely to make it into production. (*Mini*) *Below*, a Californian Moke for comparison. (*Rene Wachter*)

Future Mokes

Could the Mini Moke make a comeback? In 2009 Mini created a stir when they announced a modern 'interpretation' of the Moke. The Beachcomber concept car, a four-seater soft-top with pillar-less open sides and large alloy wheels, was unveiled in 2010 at the North American Auto Show. With 'all-wheel-drive', it has been described by Mini as a junior Sport Utility Vehicle (SUV):

> The Mini Beachcomber Concept projects the principle of the Mini Moke into the 21st century. The rustic appearance of the car and its consistent concept of consciously reducing the body components and interior to the minimum clearly follow the tradition of the radically open Mini Moke back in the 1960s.

Cutting through the hyperbole, there was a kernel of truth in the notion that the Beachcomber was indeed inspired by the Moke. Mini also pointed out that the shape of the radiator grille echoed that of the Moke's. But they could just as easily have pointed to the Austin Mini and Riley Beach Cars of the 1960s as the source of inspiration. These beach cars were produced in limited numbers as courtesy vehicles for hotels and resorts, and they also had open pillar-less sides. BMC used one to take visiting VIPs and journalists around its Longbridge site.

Bird's eye view of the Mini Beachcomber concept car. (*Mini*)

The Beachcomber concept has more in common with the Mini beach cars which were produced in small numbers for hotels and resorts. (*Pat Patterson*) *Below*, this stylish Moke has been modified to resemble the boats at St Tropez. (*Mark van Tulder*)

Mini say that the Beachcomber concept could incorporate light plastic panels to protect the roof and the sides of the car – suddenly it is beginning to sound like the Mokes of old. However, there is every likelihood that further development of the Beachcomber will be scuppered by safety regulations regarding the lack of side bracing.

A Chinese Moke?

When is a Moke not a Moke? In 2012 Moke International in Australia announced that they were building a new 'Classic' Moke in a joint venture with Chery Motors and their subsidiary Sicar Engineering in China. It was said that the vehicle will be released by mid-April 2013 with a 1,000cc engine and they have plans to produce an Electric eMoke at some point. With no direct connection to the original Mokes, this new vehicle is, in essence, another clone and whether it will be up to scratch or accepted within the Moke community remains to be seen.

(*Moke International*)

Timeline

1959   Morris Mini launched.

BMC 'Buckboard' military Moke prototypes first produced.

1962   Shorter 72.5 inch wheelbase prototype.

Twini-Moke double-engined for 4WD.

1963   80 inch wheelbase version – pilot for the civilian Moke.

1964   Mini Moke launched on British market with 850cc engine.

1966   Moke production begins in Australia on a small scale.

1967   *The Prisoner* TV series aired in UK.

Mark II introduced with second wiper, etc., also available in white.

1968   The end of UK manufacture. All production transferred to Australia where it is marketed as the Morris Mini Moke.

1972   A special export model, known as the Californian, with 1,275cc engine.

1973   Now branded as the Leyland Moke.

1975   Pick-up version introduced.

1977   Californian name resurrected with a new model featuring denim seats, spoked wheels and Roo bars.

1982   Australian production halted and the factory closed to make way for the assembly of Peugeot cars.

1983   Production began in Portugal with the first cars completed in 1984.

1986   Moke 86, a revised model.

1989   Last Portugese Moke produced.

1990   Moke name sold to the Italian company Cagiva.

1991   Production resumed in Portugal under Cagiva with the cars branded as Mokes.

1993   The end of Moke production.

2010   Mini unveiled their Beachcomber concept car.

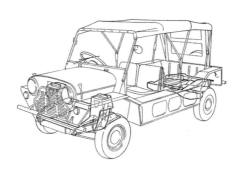

THE MINI-MOKE

B2885

Resources

Bibliography

Although the Moke featured in countless magazine articles over the years, there are very few books on the subject. Brooklands Books has published two collections of the articles: *Mini Moke 1964–1989*, compiled by Tim Nuttall, and *Mini Moke Ultimate Portfolio*, by R. M. Clarke. Some more recent articles can be found online. The Mini Moke Club has produced a number of publications including *A Guide to Mini Mokes* (1977), and there is also *Mini Moke: A Comprehensive Guide to Restoration*, by Roy Scott (2005). Both are out of print at the time of publication for this book, but updated editions might be forthcoming. Workshop manuals for the Mini, as well as the driver's handbook for the Moke, have been produced in reprint form, as have the equivalent Australian manuals. Original copies are offered on auction sites periodically and scanned versions are also available on CD.

Organisations

The Mini Moke Club www.mokeclub.org
South Australia Moke Club www.samokeclub.asn.au
Moke Owners Association of Victoria www.moke.org.au
Six of One – The Prisoner Appreciation Society www.sixofone.org.uk

The flying Moke displayed at the Haynes Motor Museum in Somerset. This is one of the prototype military Mokes intended for air dropping.

The author tries out John Walpole's 1964 Austin Mini-Moke for size.

Acknowledgements

I am very grateful to the many Moke owners who have shared their enthusiasm and allowed me to photograph their cars. In particular, my special thanks go to John Walpole and Paul Hancox. Unless otherwise stated, all new photography is by the author. Additional images have come from a number of sources and I am grateful to Campbell McCutcheon, Francis Robinson, Stephan Hacker, Trond Bremseth, CédEm, Nicolas Verhoeven, Ad Meskens, Katherine Tompkins, Sicnag, AlfvanBeem, Steve Baker, Besopha, Jim Gifford, Flying Cloud, FaceMePLS, Mrs Logic, Joost J. Bakker, Mike Gabb, Moo_Mo1, Rene Wachter, Mark van Tulder, Ken Butterfield, Pat Douglass and Pat Patterson.

Final thanks to my wife Ute for her patient proof reading and support.

'Be seeing you!'